HF406419

THE GLITCH IN THE GAME OF LIFE

COPYRIGHT

The Glitch In The Game Of Life Copyright © 2024 for Beaumont Cf LLC
https://link.me/glensky

All rights reserved. No part of this publication may be reproduced, stored, or transmitted in any form or by any means, electronic, mechanical, photocopying, recording, scanning, or otherwise, without written permission from the publisher. It is illegal to copy this book, post it to a website, or distribute it by any other means without permission.

The information here is eye-opening to the average player of the game; it is for educational purposes to level up players of the game. The publisher holds all rights to this publication. It is strictly prohibited to copy, distribute, or post this book without written permission. Any form of reproduction, whether electronic or mechanical, is strictly prohibited as well. This book is protected by law, and any unauthorized use will be prosecuted.

The publisher has worked hard to bring this book to the readers, and they deserve all the credit and recognition for their work. It is important to respect the copyright laws and honor the hard work put into this publication. Any form of piracy or unauthorized distribution is not only illegal but also unfair to the publisher and the authors.

Please be aware of the consequences of violating the copyright laws. It not only harms the publisher and authors but also sets a bad precedent for the publishing industry. Let us all work together to protect the rights of the creators and respect their hard work. Remember, with their efforts, we have access to great books like this one. Let us all play our part in promoting and supporting the creative industry.

ISBN-13: 9798873041398

DEDICATION

This book is dedicated to my mom, who taught me how powerful the mind is. Time taught me the value of life. Friends taught me true perseverance. My family taught me how to feel and care.

"Difficulties taught me that every setback is a lesson. Life moves quickly, and we can't get stuck on things that everyone will eventually forget because memories fade. The fears about what others might think will be forgotten too." Time never stops, and people are minding their own business, so are you.

This book is dedicated to somebody who is looking for their best version and mind data sets to use their most powerful tool in the game: the mind. If you master the mind, you dominate your actions. It is dedicated to those who have self-love and desire to become their best version every day. I also highlight certain patterns from the system for anybody to understand the rules of the game.

ACKNOWLEDGMENTS

"This book is not just a personal account of my experiences with 'the glitch'; it is a narrative path that connects with you, the reader. My journey wouldn't have been possible without my mom, who supported me from the beginning until I turned 16 and took control of my life, identity, beliefs, and patterns. This highlights that we are responsible for our actions and the reactions they bring."

In Colombia, I had the pleasure of being guided by Luz Dary with her company, Bioreprogramacion. She basically reprogrammed my mind to believe in myself recognizing patterns. The retreat is called "Reborn," where you die to be reborn into a better version of yourself.

I got it like a birth certificate, and I'm so thankful for all the experiences I have had in my life. Each experience shapes me in the way I am today, and all I chase is being 1% better every day. If I hadn't committed so many times, I wouldn't be doing everything I do for my community because there are glitches in the game.

TABLE OF CONTENT

CHAPTER ONE - THE GAME BEGINS

Welcome to The Game of Life, where every step is a move in the board game we all play. Imagine life as the ultimate game, with its own set of rules, challenges, and the promise of victory for those who dare to play strategically. In this chapter, we'll unravel the parallels between the games we play on our screens and the game we live in real life, showing how strategic thinking can lead to triumph.

The Game Of Life

Life is a journey where evolution is key. Picture yourself navigating through levels, each presenting its challenges and opportunities. The more you practice and engage, the more adept you become, leveling up to unlock new dimensions of success. The essence lies in the continuous pursuit of improvement by at least 1%, just like in life. Every day brings challenges and opportunities, but you decide what to focus on and where to direct your attention.

The first rule
of any game is
to know you
are in one.

Rules And Mechanics

Just as every game has its rules, so does the game of life. In the United States, where I reside, there are a myriad of rules everyone must understand and follow to succeed. These rules shape our experiences, interactions, and opportunities. From education and business choices to societal norms, comprehending the rules is the first step toward mastering the game.

Understanding the system and loopholes of the country you find yourself in is crucial. It's like playing a game in a foreign land; to succeed, you must learn and adapt to the local rules. This cultural immersion is fundamental to excelling in the diverse challenges life throws your way.

"When I first arrived in the United States, I didn't even know the language. Yet, I mastered the game to the point that I changed my status and stepped out of the system." I relinquish my citizenship to become a foreign national, a different status that lets me operate under different rules in The Game.

Remember, feedback is the only way to scale to new levels. If you don't see that you're failing, you cannot work on it. This is why I added a space at the end of each chapter for you to write down your feedback and your understanding as we see the world from similar but different perspectives. Also, in the book, I mention my path as an example of "The Glitch" because I changed my life at 16 years old by understanding the game you are about to see.

This picture above was taken when I started entrepreneurship, and since then, I have never looked back. The whole mission has been to become 1% better every day, no matter how I feel.

Level One: The Starting Point

Now, let's plunge into Level One, the starting point of our grand adventure. This is where the game begins, and the initial challenges emerge. Discipline and mindset take center stage in this first level. Much like in any game, developing discipline is akin to mastering the controls. It's the foundational skill that enables you to navigate through obstacles and seize opportunities.

Your mindset dictates how you react to situations and keeps you accountable. It is the compass guiding your journey. Level One is about understanding that discomfort is a natural part of progress. It's the price you pay for growth in advance. By embracing this discomfort and adopting a resilient mindset, you gain the tools necessary to overcome the trials that lie ahead.

I got comfortable being uncomfortable by waking up early. I used to hate waking up early because I had to do it every day for school. Now, I wake up early, start writing, and then go to the beach for 30 minutes to do some breathwork and appreciation. Let's focus on the principal values—health, family, wealth, and opportunities. Feeling blessed attracts more blessings. We are like magnets; whatever we talk about, think about, or believe is what we become. So, start by manifesting everything you want and being thankful for everything you have.

This book is your guide through Level One and beyond. It's about building your skills, leveling up your mindset, and ultimately mastering the art of playing the game of life to adapt to any situation. As we venture further, we'll uncover secrets, conquer challenges, and unlock the true potential within ourselves. The game has begun, and the journey promises to be nothing short of extraordinary success.

Your Thoughts:

This jungle was part of the retreat I went on to change my patterns, and I often find myself in nature. Just being me and feeling at home, I started from scratch here, putting new patterns in my mind.

CHAPTER TWO - Meet The Glitch

In the realm of life and business, we often find ourselves as characters navigating through a dynamic storyline. Let's embark on the journey of character creation with Glen, our protagonist, whose story embodies the essence of starting from zero every day to aim for more.

Meet Glensky Inagas, a firm believer that a change in mindset can unlock the doors to the seemingly impossible. With this simple approach, he ventured into entrepreneurship, quickly turning his ideas into a profitable reality. But Glen's story goes beyond just financial success; it's rooted in a deep commitment to supporting those in need, showing them how he did it so they can use the codes in the game the right way.

As we explore Glen's character, we discover the resilience that defines him. His journey was riddled with struggles through language, mistakes, and wrong decisions. Yet, he never succumbed to the challenges. Instead, he saw each setback as an opportunity to learn and grow. For Glen, every day presented a new chance to embrace hope and advance on the path to success because he believed in creating his luck. By waking up earlier, Glen had more hours to get ahead of himself. He fasted every morning to gain extra energy and focus. It's unusual, isn't it? This is because we all have different realities based on our daily actions. From this point, you become comfortable being uncomfortable since you want to grow most of the time.

The formula is to get uncomfortable doing things that make you better, like reading, going to the gym, or doing something that challenges you to get out of your comfort zone. Train your mind to be under pressure so it's always prepared and open-minded to learn from others and become wise, meaning making the right decisions.

Crucially, Glen recognizes the impact of mentors on his journey. He firmly believes that guided direction and support are indispensable on the road to success by the right source. His family, a wellspring of inspiration, served as a driving force when he started building his business from scratch. But that doesn't mean he was taking business advice from them because you need to identify the ultimate level and who's at that level so you can learn from the best. It wasn't just about financial success for him; it was about creating a better life for his parents and enjoying the results of his discipline and smart work.

Now, let's dig deep into the importance of building a robust foundation in your network—a cornerstone for success. Imagine your business as a game where demand and supply are the key players. A strong network not only connects you with potential clients but also lays the groundwork for growing business relationships. For Glen, connecting with people and building a network became crucial aspects of his success. He understood that having supply when there's demand is the winning strategy in the game of business.

In addition, Glen realized the importance of physical health for mental agility. He transformed his body into a machine through regular exercise, understanding that a healthy body leads to a healthy mind. The entrepreneurial lifestyle demanded peak performance, and Glen met the challenge by incorporating a commitment to physical well-being in his daily routine. This balanced approach to life, falling into his theory that improving by 1% a day will change your life in one year or two is a reminder to all of us that success is not just about work but about maintaining a healthy balance in all aspects of life, with this being said yes sometimes we tend to focus a lot on work only or lean towards something but always keep yourself grounded to find that balance to not feel overwhelmed.

Education also played a pivotal role in Glen's journey. He understood the transformative power of continuous learning in developing smart thinking. Each day presented an opportunity to acquire new knowledge and skills, contributing to his personal and professional growth. This emphasis on continuous learning reminds us that our journey to success is a never-ending process of growth and development, so always see yourself as a student, even if you are already successful. We are evolving, and staying in the learning mode would be to your advantage to adapt.

As we continue exploring The glitch character, we'll uncover more insights, challenges, and triumphs that form the tapestry of your journey. In the next chapter, we delve deeper into the game of life and business through the lens of a glitch.

Your Thoughts:

Persistence Process

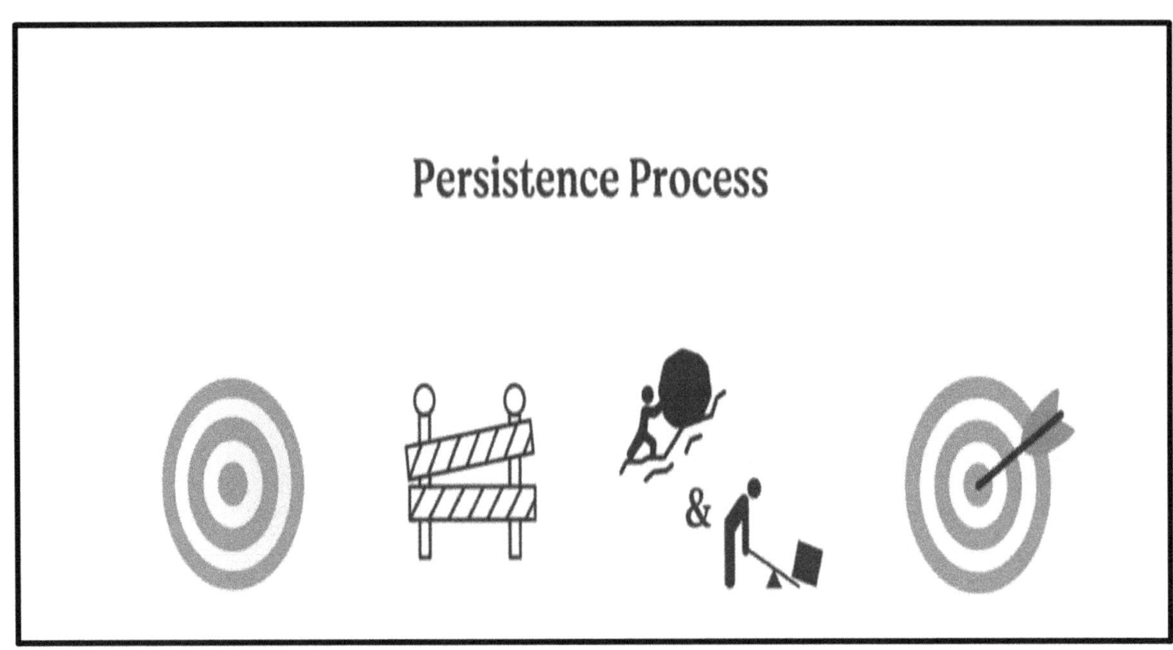

As long as we are persistent in our pursuit of our deepest destiny, we will continue to grow.

CHAPTER THREE - THE POWER OF PERSISTENCE

The Meaning Of Consistent Practice And Perseverance

Imagine you're crafting a character in your game. In this game, discipline is crucial to sculpting the best version of yourself. Forget the flashy objects or instant success stories; it's all about showing up day in and day out and putting in the effort.

But why is this so crucial? Because discipline builds character, and from character, you become the kind of person who achieves great things. We're not talking about massive leaps; we're talking about the everyday habits that may seem small but compound over time to create a formidable force.

Remember that ego sometimes gets in the way. The ego is the part of our thinking that believes we're better than anyone or that we know it all. Be conscious of it and humble yourself to learn from everyone around you.

Story Time: From Consistent Education To Business Growth

Allow me to share a personal story. I've been committed to being consistent in my education, fitness, and goals and resisting distractions for an extended period. Did it pay off? Absolutely. This is called delayed gratification. This simple act of focusing on learning without getting sidetracked became the backbone of my business growth.

It's a testament to the power of consistent effort. This is the mindset we all need to have. When I mention mindset, I mean you need to start believing it. Like the saying, "fake it until you make it," but also take action to turn those dreams into reality.

Incremental Progress Through Daily Practice

Now, let's break down the daily practice into actionable steps. No, it doesn't involve doing something monumental every day. We're talking about small, manageable actions that add up over time. Remember, 1% a day is 365 percent a year.

❖ **Waking Up Early:**

- Start with something as fundamental as waking up early—from 4 a.m. to 6 a.m. This gives you a head start on the day. Trust me, it's a game-changer. You get more hours than the average person, setting the tone for productivity.

- Imagine waking up, washing your face, and going for a walk to start connecting with yourself. Take this time to appreciate life, family, health, the sun, food, a roof over your head, water, friends, and many other blessings. In your life, I'm personally grateful for my stepdad; thanks to him, I'm legal in the United States. Small things like that might be huge for someone else, which is why we have to appreciate and recognize our blessings, no matter how big or small.

- It takes time to get used to doing this, but we need to get creative and enjoy the process. Do not make it hard, but enjoy waking up early to work on yourself because you are the main character in this game. Taking care of your body, mind, and soul is essential for your character to perform at its best.

❖ **Mindset Matters:**

- Begin your day with the right mindset. Take a walk, breathe in the fresh air, or clear your mind for at least 15 minutes to set the tone of your day. Since we live in a world that keeps us distracted, it's important to start the day focused. While you're at it, start saying thanks and think about the things you're grateful for. This isn't just some new-age positivity talk; it's about attracting abundance and recognizing your blessings every day to start the day in abundance.

- Your mind is a magnet. If you start the day by giving your mind positive thoughts, it will power this Machine of yours to attract anything you want in life. Grounding could be even more powerful while you do this, as I do at the beach every morning, because grounding is in the natural ground, like Grass or Sand.

- Your mindset is the way you think and approach situations, so for me, every time I approach a situation, I have the mindset of a winner. No matter what, I never give up; just like Napoleon Hills said, "Victory is always possible for the person who refuses to stop fighting."

❖ **Gratitude For Abundance:**
- Gratitude isn't just a feel-good concept; it attracts abundance. When you focus on the things you're thankful for, you send out positive energy to the universe. It's like programming your mind for success because all you can think of is positive, and that's what your mind will focus on.

- We all have situations in our lives, but the way we react to them can make a big difference. Approaching situations with positive thinking can help you figure out helpful ways to solve them.

Your Homework: The 21-Day Goal

Now, here's where your character meets the road to success. I challenge you to start on a 21-day journey of consistent practice. It's simple, but it requires commitment.

Here's your roadmap:

- ❖ **Day 1-7: Waking Up Early**
  - Set a goal to wake up 30 minutes earlier than your usual time every day. Use this time for reflection, planning, or light exercise. Wait to use your phone until 8 a.m. Let's be honest: You only need it then to start work or catch up on emails and start worrying about bills or any notification it has for you, but until then, set the tone of that day, don't let your phone dictate how you feel when you wake up.

- ❖ **Day 8-14: Mindset Matters**
  - Incorporate time with yourself—"no phone or distractions"—into your routine. Practice mindfulness, express gratitude, and visualize your goals for the day. This can be as simple as writing down things to get done in the morning or at night. Find time for you to organize on the inside, and you will see how everything gets organized on the outside.

- ❖ **Day 15-21: Gratitude for Abundance**
  - Keep a gratitude journal. Each morning, write down ten new things you're thankful for. Notice the positive shift in your life like the prior examples.

Key Takeaway

Consistent practice and perseverance aren't reserved for a select few. Anyone can embrace these principles and start building a character that leads to success. It's about the small, daily actions that compound over time, creating a powerful force that propels you toward your goals.

Completing the 21-day goal will not only cultivate discipline but also lay the foundation for your character's evolution. In the next chapter, we delve deeper into the intricacies of the game, uncovering more gems to make your journey a success, one step at a time.

Your Thoughts:

CHAPTER FOUR - UNLOCKING NEW LEVELS

Facing Solo Moments: Navigating Level Two Obstacles

Once you realize that your mind is the most powerful tool you have, Develop the mind and optimize it by keeping it safe from negative spaces. By being with yourself, only allowing your divine energy to flow thoughts through your mind and make them reality is powerful, just like everything in the world was thought before being created.

The mind is where belief starts to happen and also where you hold memories that are attached to your feelings, so understand that you have control at all times if you have control of the mind by doing breathwork. This way, you learn how to trick your mind, just like I did this by believing in myself not only to breathe of course, but also by affirmations through taking constant action. Now that I have accomplished most of my goals, I have to keep increasing my goals.

To unlock new levels, you will face adversity—you're on your own. This could be a bit frustrating, but do not fear! It's an opportunity to harness your inner strength and take charge. Imagine Level Two obstacles as situations where your decisions matter the most. Controlling your habits and cultivating a sharp mindset make you become the pro of this game by saying no to fun activities that aren't aligned with your vision.

In my personal experience, being alone is good so that I can focus on my stuff. Of course, I would love to be with my family more than anything since they live in Venezuela, but I see the positive side of it. I can focus on my stuff, so I have no excuse. Understand that we all have situations, but if you really want something, it's up to you.

Adapting Strategies For Higher Levels

Just like in the era of the internet, success often hides in adaptation. Leveling up requires recognizing that the Game is evolving as human beings, and so should your strategies. The digital age has transformed the way we live and work. Those who adapted are thriving, and those who didn't are playing catch-up. Being comfortable with discomfort is a crucial aspect of this journey to level up quicker. Think of it as upgrading your character—each adaptation is like adding a new skill to your records.

Please think about AI. "It was a major trend in 2022, and leveraging such trends can make you more efficient because it signifies progress." So, we need to adapt and thrive in this trend.

Experience Points (XP) Through Practice

Now, let's talk about gaining experience points (XP). In The Game Of Life, XP is earned through practice in real-life encounters. Remember, everyone starts as a student, but through continuous practice, you accumulate XP and level up. Just like in a video game, where characters gain expertise by confronting challenges, life rewards those who consistently strive for improvement.

It doesn't mean you have to change your life tomorrow, but as little as 1 percent today is enough to evolve in the Game. To become a Master of the game, you have to do more than 1 percent, but as little as that is enough for you to move towards your goals like I did with mine, "Glitches."

Picture this: every action, every challenge overcome, and every skill acquired is like earning XP. The more you practice, the more XP you accumulate. It's the secret sauce to becoming a master in any field. Whether you're learning a new skill, honoring your craft, or navigating the challenges of Life, remember that practice is your gateway to mastery. Embrace the process while you gather those XP points, and watch as you unlock new levels of your higher self.

If you become a master of rejection, you will be able to talk to anybody with experience. It's easy for you because you fail so many times trying it out. By one year, trying it for 30 minutes a day, you will be a Master in any sales job or network marketing position.

So, as you navigate Level Two, remember to stick with your purpose, adapt to changing situations, and gather as many XP points as you can. Failing and being uncomfortable will boost your XP because you learn from failing, gaining experience, and each step forward brings you closer to unlocking the next level.

Your Thoughts:

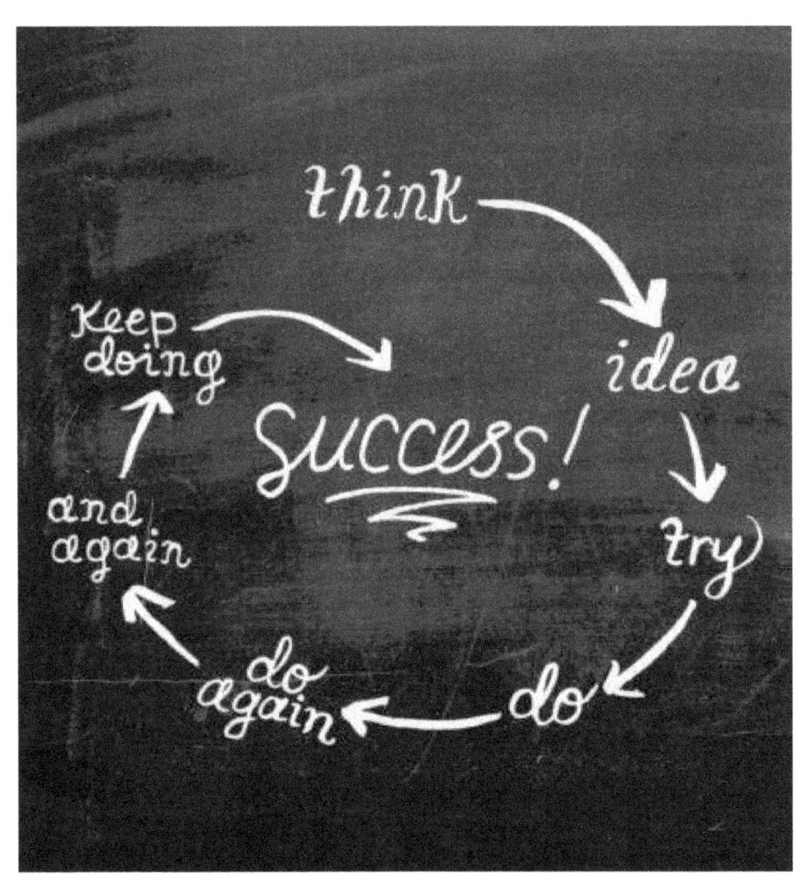

think
idea
try
do
do again
and again
keep doing
Success!

CHAPTER 5 - EMBRACING FAILURE

Understanding Failure as Part of the Game

In the game of life, unlike traditional games where you receive rewards for winning, failure is your valuable currency to level up. Embrace failure just as you do with winning because each setback is an opportunity for growth. Think of it as earning experience points (XP) every time you encounter a setback. It might seem hard, but this situation builds your character, making you stronger for bigger challenges.

Failing is a vital part of the learning process. Just as in games where you gather resources to level up, each failure brings you one step closer to the next level of experience. I recommend you do things you are scared of failing at because that's the only way you will have a life full of stories and experiences. In this game, there are winners and lessons learned.

Resilience: Bouncing Back From Setbacks

Now, let's talk about the crucial skill of resilience. When you encounter failures—and you will—it's essential to measure them not by their impact on your self-worth but by the lessons they bring. Imagine you're a character in a game who gets knocked down but bounces back stronger each time. Resilience is a superpower.

To train your mind and body for resilience, consider incorporating practices like meditation, yoga, or even boxing into your routine. Learning from your own mistakes through exercise and watching feedback is very important to actually getting better at anything. These activities not only help you stay physically fit but also cultivate mental strength. Just as a character leveled up their skills to face tougher challenges, these practices empowered them to tackle the obstacles life throws their way.

Learning From The Pros: Stories Of Overcoming Failure

Now, let's draw inspiration from famous players in the game of life who faced failures but ultimately emerged victorious:

Michael Jordan

Even the legendary Michael Jordan, often hailed as the greatest basketball player of all time, encountered failure. He missed over 9,000 shots in his career, lost almost 300 games, and missed the game-winning shot 26 times. Yet, he used these failures as stepping stones to greatness, ultimately winning six NBA championships.

What set Jordan apart wasn't just his unparalleled talent but his unwavering determination in the face of adversity. Each setback fueled a fire within him, igniting a relentless drive to improve and succeed. Instead of dwelling on past failures, Jordan used them as motivation to push himself harder, train longer, and elevate his game to new heights.

Today, Michael Jordan's legacy extends far beyond the basketball court. His resilience in the face of failure serves as a beacon of hope and inspiration for countless individuals striving to overcome their challenges. Jordan's story reminds us that failure isn't the end of the road; it's merely a stepping stone on the journey to greatness.

In the end, it was Jordan's resilience—his ability to embrace failure, learn from it, and use it as fuel for success—that propelled him to become the greatest basketball player of all time. His story is a testament to the power of resilience and serves as a timeless reminder that greatness is not achieved in spite of failure but because of it.

J.K. Rowling

Before the immense success of the Harry Potter series, J.K. Rowling faced rejection from multiple publishers. She went from being a struggling single mother to one of the wealthiest and most influential authors in the world. Her resilience and belief in her story eventually led to unparalleled success.

Embracing failure wasn't a sign of weakness for Rowling; it was a testament to her strength of character and unwavering belief in her craft. With each setback, she honed her skills, refined her narrative voice, and fortified her resolve to share her story with the world.

Through her journey, Rowling teaches us a profound lesson: failure is not the end but a necessary waypoint on the path to greatness. It's a crucible in which resilience is tempered and perseverance is forged. By embracing failure, we unlock the door to boundless potential, turning obstacles into opportunities and setbacks into stepping stones.

The Iconic Comeback: My Personal Story

I have experienced numerous failures to the point where it felt like life was ending, but there's always a good point of view in these situations. Getting uncomfortable and doing those things that scare you—this is real success—when it's earned, not given.

Quick Story

When I was building my service business at 19 years old, I had a motorcycle accident that left me bedridden for three months, only able to walk with a back brace. Fortunately, I had enough demand to hire my first employee, so I did because I had no choice.

I was frustrated because I couldn't do things myself, but when my business was booming, I was the head of the business, taking care of growth while my employees took care of client retention.

The lesson of the story is that I faced a life-threatening situation and then had to make an important decision. With a resilient mindset, I kept up with the situation, feeling very grateful to be alive and learning at the same time. I never stopped reading or educating myself because that was the only way to stay ready for the next opportunity. In this life, success is based on the opportunities you build up for yourself, not luck but hard work.

Your Thoughts:

CHAPTER SIX - BUILDING A SUPPORT SYSTEM

Unlocking Success with Mentors

Think of mentors as your personal strategy guides in the game of life. They're like experienced players who've been through the levels, faced challenges, and know the shortcuts. Finding the right mentor is like discovering a cheat code that helps you navigate the game more efficiently. It's not just about learning from their professional success; it's also about understanding their daily actions. Different inputs lead to different outcomes.

The first step is to find a mentor you admire, someone successful in your field. Make sure to do your research on these mentors to avoid bad experiences. Look at how they operate their business, adopt their positive habits, and learn from their failures. Good artists copy; great artists steal. It's like upgrading the winning moves of a skilled player, creating a better version of your mentor.

The Trio of Mentors

In life, having a trio of mentors can be a game-changer. Here's the breakdown:

1. **The Expert Mentor:** This is the seasoned pro—the best in the game. Learn from their vast experience and gain insights into the strategies that led to their success.

- **Think about it:** If you could spend time with someone you know in your industry, learning from their experience through conversation, wouldn't that be valuable to you? I spend a lot of my time with the greatest people I learn from, and I execute right away.

2. **The Peer Mentor:** Connect with someone who is at the same level as you. This mentor becomes your ally, a partner to share victories, defeats, and the day-to-day experiences of the journey.

- Imagine a best friend with the same mindset, desires, and goals—someone at the same level as you, not more successful or less successful—like a soulmate aligned with your vision, you could call it. It might be your partner because it's someone you share a lot of experiences with. They are basically your mirror, teaching you to see your weaknesses and lacking spots and also celebrating in those solo times when you are focused.

3. **The Mentee:** Pay attention to the power of being a mentor yourself. Teaching someone else what you've learned not only helps them but also reinforces your knowledge and skills.

I created Glitches, a community to share everyone's experience in business, investing and networking. I did it to have someone under me so I could teach and retain more information. Everyone with a brain is powerful, so don't underestimate someone just because they don't have the same results. Staying humble and helping someone can open many doors for you.

Navigating the Mentorship Game

Step 1: Clear Vision

Before approaching a mentor, have a clear vision of your goals and who you are as a person. A mentorship should be a relationship where both parties learn from each other and provide value to each other. Knowing what you want to achieve helps you pick the right mentor aligned with your aspirations.

It only takes one person to change your life, but you need to have a clear vision, the right mindset, and the courage to get uncomfortable and grow every day. Do that thing you really like doing only some days and develop a clear vision. Every mentor will ask if you have something figured out, so don't just rely on them.

A mentor will keep you accountable if they see you are trying but have your guard down. A mentor won't babysit because it's a professional relationship of mutual benefit and respect.

Step 2: Be Valuable

Approach a potential mentor when you have something valuable to offer. It could be a skill, a unique perspective, or a solution that can replace a task they are currently handling. Try to figure out what they are lacking to make it easier. Many people need to be more relaxed and caught up in the day-to-day to even check how they can improve their lives. If you can contribute value by optimizing their life, you are ahead of the game. I have done this with several mentors, where I provide value with my Marketing or content creation skills to surround myself with the best in the field I want to be in.

Quick Story:

When I started going to the gym in Sunny Isles, I met my boxing coach, Gil Reyes, who is a pro fighter. I provided value by creating content for him, and in return, he gave me boxing lessons. We started training, and now we are super close. I've become his number one student, training with pros. Similarly, I met my real estate mentor at an event, got my license, and now I can sell real estate, building my network around successful people in the field I'm pursuing.

I've done this repeatedly to learn a little of everything, ultimately aiming to create my community focused on growth rather than money. It doesn't matter if you started yesterday or have been doing this for years—we are all powerful and need discipline taught through mindset.

I'm just a normal Venezuelan who came to the United States with my mom and started working jobs to pay for my car, rent, food, and other expenses. I changed my mindset at 17 years old to become the best version of myself. Now, I am a Foreign National, business owner, and investor in crypto and real estate, and more opportunities are coming my way. I position my close people in the right rooms by creating my community, focusing on educational and networking spaces. We have levels of entry: a free one for starters, then Glitch members who learn about Structure & Real Estate through self-education and get inside information about crypto developments.

Step 3: Time Is Precious

Understand that time is the most precious resource we have since it doesn't stop. Taking care of your time and having good time management skills are vital to maintaining a schedule of high performance, constant growth and proper sleep time to recover and keep performing.

Timing is vital because the quicker you can make decisions, the quicker you move into life goals, deals, and situations. Like a game of chess, you only need to make a few moves as the king by thinking your moves ahead. To be at the top of the game, you must have a team to make only a few moves like the king. Think about having a chauffeur and a Chef to save you time so you, as the king, only focus on high-value moves to keep staying at the top of your own game.

Have in mind that going through problems yourself will take some time while you figure out the situation, then try and error; instead of trying to get a mentor's experience to let them help you since they have already been through it, offer value in exchange when approaching a Mentor have figured out what they are lacking and bring up a solution that automatically feels like they owe you something so have a skill or solution that can save them time or enhance their efficiency making you valuable for them and using it as a currency to get their time.

I learned about marketing and content creation by accident, investing in my brand. I got a whole experience that taught me all about digital media. Because of that, I have value in something everyone is using nowadays to have a Brand online. So, I use that to connect with people in real estate or fitness stuff. I exchange my value for someone's value, "
XP."

Remember, mentors are not just sources of advice; they are guides on your journey like a Godfather. In the next chapter, we'll explore real-life stories of successful mentorship and how these relationships can propel you forward in this game. Get ready to level up your support system!

Your Thoughts:

CHAPTER SEVEN - LEARNING FROM THE MASTERS

Mastering Wisdom: The Power To Level Up

In this game of life, understanding the concept of a master player is your responsibility. These players can learn from everyone around them, not only from those above but also from those below. I call it wisdom. It's earned by making mistakes and learning from them so you know what is the correct move. But what if I told you that you could learn like the masters by talking to others in their industry or their area of interest? That's how they became masters of the game—by learning from other players' failures since failure always leaves a lesson.

Think of wisdom as the ultimate power-up. This can guide you through challenges that you don't have to experience yourself and make the right decisions. Being a glitch player, someone who finds loopholes in real life by surrounding themselves with masters is the real glitch. It saves time going through trial and error to become a master of your own game. It's a journey that takes time: dropping your ego, accepting yourself, and learning from others.

All Students Are Equal, But Some Are Masters

Now, imagine everyone in life as a student—you, me, and everyone else. We are all students, even the masters, who need to be students to become masters. We all share the same basic components: legs, arms, and a big computer inside our heads. This metaphor signifies that, at the core, we're all the same, but the way we think or react to situations is completely different. Our belief system is influenced by the people we grow up with. If you figure out at a young age who you want to be, it's easier to identify who to learn from because, in the end, we all have big goals, and we're working towards achieving them. The key lesson here is that anything that doesn't contribute to our goals is a distraction that steals our time. The master players understand this, and they use their time wisely since the clock doesn't stop.

Stories Of Known Players

Let's look at some known players who have achieved great success. Picture them as characters in a game – just like you and me. They faced challenges and had setbacks, and yet they emerged as champions or success stories. What sets them apart? It's their commitment and discipline to their goals and their ability to make wise decisions. These players didn't waste time on things that didn't align with their objectives because they had a clear vision, and whatever was not helping them grow in the game was probably killing them.

Kobe's Drive

- **Early Inspiration:** Even as a young player, Kobe identified legends like Magic Johnson, Larry Bird, and Michael Jordan as his mentors. He devoured footage, studied their techniques, and even called them up, seeking advice. Michael Jordan, in particular, became his "big brother," a source of guidance and motivation.

- **Learning from the Best:** Kobe wasn't just mimicking; he was analyzing. He understood that emulating greatness wasn't enough. He had to dissect their skills, understand the "why" behind their moves, and then incorporate them into his own game, making them his own.

- **Relentless Work Ethic:** Kobe's work ethic was legendary. The infamous "Kobe workout" stories detail his pre-dawn training sessions, pushing himself beyond perceived limits. This dedication wasn't just about physical conditioning; it was about mastering his craft and becoming intimately familiar with every aspect of the game.

- **Always Learning:** Kobe never stopped learning. Even at the peak of his career, he sought out new coaches, trainers, and even players to glean knowledge from. He understood that the game was constantly evolving, and so did his approach to it.

Key Takeaway:

Kobe Bryant's story is a testament to the transformative power of mentorship and becoming a student of the game. By actively seeking guidance from those who have walked the path before him, analyzing their successes and failures, and constantly striving to learn and improve, Kobe ascended to the pinnacle of his sport.

Lessons and Tricks

- **Get the Right Mentor:**
  - ❖ Choosing the right character you want to be in the game and selecting the right mentor is crucial. Sometimes, we find ourselves doing the same things our family or friends are doing, but it might not be our true passion or align with our life's vision. Everything falls into place when you figure out your vision, like a GPS guiding you to your goals. Having the right mentor accelerates this process since they have been in this situation before. If you are building a project but your vision needs to be clearer, you might be wasting your time.

  - ❖ Working hard as immigrants in the system takes so much Time and Energy from us, so we are too tired to question ourselves or be creative thinkers, our brains foggy from the poison we do to ourselves. A mentor is this new family member you will have to take care of like he's taking care of you.

- **Align Actions with Goals:**
  - ❖ Every action you take should align with your goals. Master players don't waste time on activities that don't contribute to their success. Be intentional about how you spend your time and energy. Once you get a crystal clear vision, every action has a meaning, and you know time is running. For example, last year, I started waking up earlier to write this book. I did it with an intention since, during the day, I'm dealing with clients or work; I figured from 4 Am to 6 Am, I'm the most creative, and I get extra hours.

- **Embrace Wise Decision-Making:**
  - ❖ Wisdom is your superpower. Learn to make decisions that align with your goals and values. Each decision you make is a step toward Winning or Losing in The Game of Life.

As you absorb these lessons, remember that you're not alone in this Game. We're all students of life, even the most successful people, who are constantly learning because this is a journey of lessons where you learn all the time. The wisdom shared by the masters is a path to help you navigate the challenges and Victories that lie ahead. Embrace the power of wisdom, align your actions with your goals, and get ready to fast-track levels in the extraordinary Game of Life with the right mentor.

I founded Glitches, a community for entrepreneurs to learn deeply about the system they are in, the basics like level 1 for free and advanced information level 2 inside the membership. We run the inner circle only allowed by the elites, those students of life that make $1M+ a year to mastermind and share the XP because once you prove you're capable of creating a vehicle making $1M+, I know you will value other elites, Only you know what it takes to level up in your game.

Your Thoughts:

47

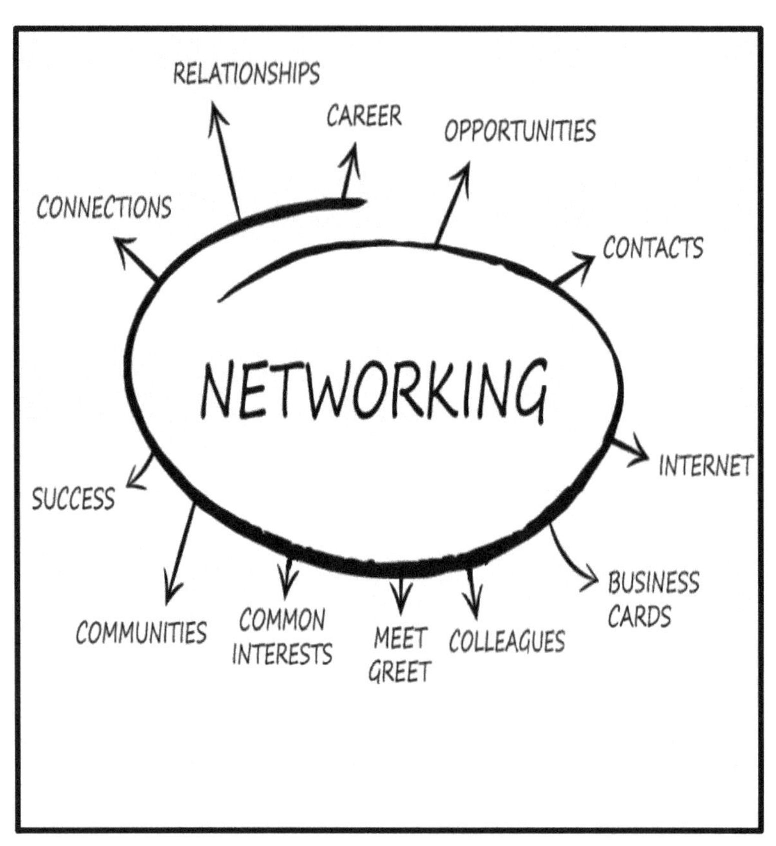

RELATIONSHIPS
CAREER
OPPORTUNITIES
CONNECTIONS
CONTACTS
NETWORKING
INTERNET
SUCCESS
BUSINESS CARDS
COMMUNITIES
COMMON INTERESTS
MEET GREET
COLLEAGUES

CHAPTER EIGHT - NETWORKING POWER

The Power of Networking

In the Game of Life, networking is what takes you to the right mentor and the right partnerships. It's not about collecting friends; it's about connecting with the right people who share your vision. Imagine your network as a team of superheroes, each with unique abilities that complement each other to become an unbeatable team.

This team needs to be built around trust and genuine connection. Build real relationships with other powerful players in the same game you are playing. Before you meet these people, manifest the right players on your team by writing down in detail who they are. Talk about it in the present tense, as if it has already happened.

Importance Of Networking

Why is networking so crucial? Wealthy people, just like superheroes, have big situations that often come with heavy price tags. When you connect with the right individuals, those with aligned visions and ambitious goals, you position yourself as a problem solver. And guess what? Problem-solving is a skill that people are willing to pay big bucks for.

Building Your Dream Team

As I mentioned before, you need to have a clear vision before stepping into building this team. Every time you meet someone, it's intentional because you know crystal clear what you want, making it easier to know who will align perfectly with you. Building relationships and trust is very important. Be authentic and genuine with the individuals in your network, potentially in your "Team," to the point where these people can send you one hundred grand without a contract. That's the level of trust I'm talking about. Keep in mind that this happens daily; just because you haven't done it doesn't mean it can't be done.

Strategies For Building A Strong And Diverse Network

1. **Give Before You Ask:** Imagine you were invited for dinner. You wouldn't show up empty-handed and expect to leave with a full plate, right? Similarly, in networking, always offer value before asking for something. It could be your time, expertise, or a simple favor like introducing a person on your team who can provide the solution to their needs. This sets the stage for meaningful connections; I call this connecting dots by providing value.

2. **Be A Genuine Listener:** When engaging with others, put on your superhero listening ears. Pay attention to their needs, challenges, and aspirations. People appreciate someone who genuinely cares. Before you jump into your agenda, take the time to understand theirs, and figure out how you can provide them value instead of taking it right away.

3. **Quality Over Quantity:** It's about something more than having a thousand contacts in your phone, although this can work if you build a CRM to keep track of every single contact. It's about having a few meaningful connections. Invest your time and energy wisely in building relationships with the right players who align with your goals and values.

Success Story from Glen

I learned about networking when I was little because my dad had connections in Venezuela for everything. He taught me the basics of it by being respectful and genuine with people to create relationships. Being good-looking was an advantage since many people judge by how you look or dress. Now that I'm older, I can say that I have mastered the art of networking by being able to talk to anyone about anything—it could be money or sports, you name it. Not only can I talk to anyone, but I can also provide value to anyone at the table.

Mastering networking unlocked my ability to talk to anyone, anywhere. By 21 years old, I already had two different partnerships in one of my businesses. It's a game-changer because when you get the right people on your team, you can go far. If you are alone, you can go fast. If you know how to balance both, you will grow fast and steadily with the right team.

Leveraging Your Network for Success

Let's take a look at real-life players who mastered the art of networking:

1. **Juan Fernando Franco and Ivan Martinez**

The Connectors: Meet Juan Fernando Franco and Ivan Martinez, the dynamic duo of network marketing whose journey from small beginnings to industry titans is nothing short of inspiring. Juan, armed with a passion for connecting with people, and Ivan, fueled by his relentless drive for success, embarked on their network marketing odyssey with humble beginnings.

Their secret? It wasn't just about selling products; it was about building genuine relationships. Juan's innate ability to empathize and truly understand the needs of others, coupled with Ivan's strategic vision and unwavering determination, formed the perfect synergy.

They didn't just wait for opportunities; they created them. Whether it was hosting engaging events, leveraging social media platforms, or simply striking up conversations with strangers, Juan and Ivan were always one step ahead. They understood that networking wasn't just about making contacts; it was about nurturing those connections and adding value to people's lives.

But their journey wasn't without its challenges. Rejections, setbacks, and moments of self-doubt tested their resolve. Yet, each obstacle only fueled their determination to succeed. They saw every setback as an opportunity to learn and grow, honing their skills and refining their approach along the way.

Through perseverance, Juan and Ivan not only achieved their financial freedom but also empowered countless others to do the same. Their story serves as a testament to the transformative power of networking—a skill that, with dedication and practice, anyone can master.

1. **Albert Einstein**

The Problem Solver: Albert Einstein, one of history's most celebrated thinkers, epitomizes the essence of a problem solver. His legendary intellect and innovative approach to scientific inquiry not only reshaped our understanding of the cosmos but also provided a blueprint for effective problem-solving in any domain.

Einstein's method was multifaceted, but at its core lay a relentless pursuit of curiosity. He approached problems with an insatiable hunger to understand the underlying principles governing the universe. This insatiable curiosity led him to ask questions that others hadn't even considered, propelling him to explore unconventional avenues of thought. His famous thought experiments, such as imagining himself riding on a beam of light, exemplify this willingness to challenge the status quo and entertain radical ideas.

Furthermore, Einstein possessed a remarkable ability to simplify complex issues. He had a special skill for distilling intricate concepts down to their essential components, enabling him to see patterns and connections that eluded others. This talent for abstraction allowed him to break down seemingly insurmountable problems into more manageable tasks, facilitating his problem-solving process.

Einstein's approach was also characterized by his willingness to embrace failure and iterate upon his ideas. He understood that setbacks were an inevitable part of the creative process and saw each obstacle as an opportunity for growth. Rather than becoming discouraged by failure, he viewed it as a valuable source of feedback, guiding him toward novel solutions.

Moreover, Einstein was a master collaborator, recognizing the importance of leveraging diverse perspectives to tackle complex problems. He surrounded himself with a network of fellow intellectuals and scientists, engaging in lively discussions and debates that fueled his creative spark. By fostering an environment of open dialogue and intellectual exchange, which I call Masterminding, he refined his ideas and pushed the boundaries of scientific inquiry.

The key takeaway from Einstein's problem-solving prowess is that it is a skill accessible to all, regardless of background or expertise. By cultivating curiosity, embracing failure, simplifying complexity, and fostering collaboration, individuals can unlock their potential to tackle challenges and drive innovation in any field. Einstein's legacy serves as a testament to the transformative power of relentless curiosity and unconventional thinking, inspiring generations to push the boundaries of what is possible through the art of problem-solving.

Conclusion

In this game of life, your network is your secret weapon. It's not about how many people you know but how well you know them, and they know you. By aligning yourself with those who share your vision and consistently providing value, you'll unlock a world of possibilities. So, put on your networking cape, venture forth, and start building connections that will shape your extraordinary journey.

Your Thoughts:

SUPPORT
PREPARATION
GOAL
OVERCOME
CHALLENGE
ACCEPTED
MISSION
MOTIVATION
SUCCESS

CHAPTER NINE - OVERCOMING CHALLENGES

Understanding The Obstacles:

This Game is filled with obstacles, and players, just like you, encounter various obstacles similar to hard times. These challenges may include the need to work hard or battle with your mind. But remember, every challenge serves a purpose and lesson, like being uncomfortable when you face new challenges. Just imagine the situations an Alpha Male must go through to get the results he gets. "Nothing is given; Everything is earned."

To be at the highest level you want to be, you must be uncomfortable and seek constant growth by doing what others are not willing to do. This comes with difficulties, but guess what? You are also learning how to overcome these obstacles by becoming resourceful. Like many entrepreneurs, we are problem solvers.

Strategies For Overcoming Challenges:
1. Meditation and Isolation Time:

- Take a moment to sit down, relax, and clear your mind. Meditation helps you gain control over your thoughts and emotions. Spending time alone, like going out to eat by yourself, is a simple yet powerful way to understand your thoughts and build confidence.

- In entrepreneurship, we get stressed out a lot, either because we have too many things or because we don't have too much to do and need to know how to bring more traffic to our business. If you search on the internet about isolation, it will say many bad things. Still, in reality, if you understand that being by yourself in a place where you feel comfortable to think and be creative is good, it's good to identify it and use it to your convenience.

- Being away from everyone is okay if you have a purpose for greatness. Go with paper and pencil to write down your thoughts because, at that moment and time, you will use your most powerful asset: your mind. You need to listen closely because the answer to the obstacles is within you.

2. Delaying Gratification:

- The ability to delay gratification is a superpower. Instead of opting for immediate rewards, consider the long-term benefits. This could mean putting in extra hours for a project or resisting the urge for instant pleasures. It's about keeping your eyes on the bigger prize.

- We, the people, tend to seek shiny objects or experiences, and we unconsciously place obstacles in our way because of those shiny experiences. We think we are missing out, but in reality, we are delaying our process, so stay focused and reward yourself later, not all the time, just like when you were a kid, and they let you play after doing your homework, but this time you reward yourself.

3. Keeping Your Word:

- Make promises to yourself and stick to them. If you decide to start a business, commit to it. These builds trust in yourself and your abilities. It's telling yourself, "I will do this," and then making it happen. Your word to yourself is as important as your word to others.
- This is why I believe in "fake it until you make it." The right way to do this is to be real like I started my business, and I didn't know anything about being an entrepreneur. Still, I really believed in myself, so I told everyone about my business and how I was getting clients even though

I didn't have any. By telling others, I was putting pressure on myself to go out there and put my mind to figure it out to get clients; also, I was using the law of attraction by talking about it. Definitely works if you know how to use it.

Inspiring Stories Of Triumph:

Let's plunge into inspiring My stories of facing adversity and emerging victoriously:

1. **Starting a Solo Business:**

❖ Imagine deciding to start a business all by yourself. You have this incredible business idea, and the only person you need to convince is yourself. This journey requires determination, hard work, and a strong belief in your abilities.

❖ Well, this is how I started my dog service business. I knew I could do it but didn't know how, so I started by choosing a sticky name, "Dukepaws," and from there, offering the service to everyone in the neighborhood with flyers I bought for 50 dollars, but nobody actually called me for that. In the meantime, I was learning about marketing and sales because I knew that was the core of the business's "cashflow," and how did I get cash flow if I didn't have clients? Well, marketing.

❖ I started my Marketing & Branding journey thanks to my business, so I started applying the basics like getting a website and doing SEO (search engine optimization) in Google. I learned everything about its keywords, so I also had to learn about psychology to think like my clients and exactly what they are looking for when they need our service. It was quite simple the keywords for a dog walker and pet sitting, so I called my business "Dukepaws dog walker and pet pitting." Ranking top 1 around the area we serve in most search engines in the world, and I accomplished getting memberships around my area to the point of making 6 figures a month.

❖ With that being said, I started this project completely from zero. I mean, like, I was 18 years old and had just moved back to my parent's house to "Attend college " when, in reality, I started a business and believed in myself. To be honest, I don't regret it because it was a flip; I did in my life but definitely had a lot of obstacles and one of the biggest ones: my business partner leaving with all my clients, and I signed him out because supposedly he had another opportunity for something else. I had to start from zero to hero, and yes, it could be frustrating, but this is how entrepreneurship goes.

❖ Now, I have new partners that take care of Dukepaws clients and memberships, also they are interested in the company's growth. I learned how to not worry about the things I can't control, like literally, there's no point in putting my energy into something that is not going to change.

2. **New Real Estate Era :**

◆ Imagine you have a beautiful business and a partner taking care of it. You start your real estate career by getting your license and starting as a Broker. Now, present yourself to this person who could help you with your real estate needs.

◆ When my business partner left, it was a setback for me, but I kept my head up to continue on the journey. Now, I'm renting cars I own, have my business with a partnership and continue to do Real Estate. So, imagine all it took for me to believe in myself and consistency because in a matter of two years, I was taking little vacations here and there but fully committed to personal growth and business growth in general.

❖ "How I perform is how my business is going to perform because I am the engine of it. Taking it to the next level is my responsibility..." Once you understand this and focus on growing, meaning your business and everything around you is growing. Now that I write and work from home, I do the work of connecting with new people out there, but in social media, where I could be in many places at the same time, so by getting a problem, all I focus on is the solution. I know it sounds easy, but our mind is too used to it to play games, and we really have control if we understand the mind.

We tend to have the idea that obstacles are annoying, or you simply don't enjoy them. Still, the truth is when you go through these moments of suffering, because it's hard, but the lessons are wonderful to grow. The idea is that you enjoy these moments as well, so take a moment to analyze the situation and understand it's a lesson, so you're paying attention, taking notes or getting xp so learn that bad times are just like good times but learning a lesson.

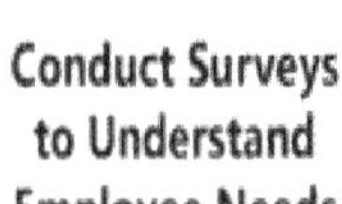

Conduct Surveys
to Understand
Employee Needs

Creating Awareness
Among
Employees

Flexible
Working Options

Paid Time off
for Important
Life Events

CHAPTER TEN - BALANCE WORK AND LIFE

The Balance Point:

Let's start with a fundamental truth: Success is not a sprint; it's a marathon. Imagine reaching the pinnacle of your dreams only to find yourself too sick to enjoy it. What's the point of embarking on this incredible journey if you end up successful but need more time to savor it? That's where the magic of balance comes into play.

In reality, most of us focus on the price we have to pay to obtain freedom. We sacrifice our time, health, and family to become the "big deal." Balance the weight of these sacrifices so they don't consume you entirely into work.

Efficient Time Management

Managing time effectively is crucial in the game. Think of your time as a valuable resource that needs careful handling. To maximize it, grab a pen and start breaking down your activities. Begin with your most important task—the one that will bring you closer to your goals. This simple act of prioritizing keeps you on track and prevents time from slipping away like sand through your fingers.

We need to use time in our favor by preparing for the day and not skipping our daily habits. The idea is to take advantage of the same twenty-four hours we all have. By preparing for the day, such as setting a to-do list the prior night, you ensure that your day is organized and productive.

Time never stops. You know this, but you can't stop it. Being organized will pay off in productivity, enabling you to take more meetings or get more done. This is the name of the efficient game: outworking the competition while also safeguarding time for yourself and your family.

The ABCs Of Self-Care

Picture yourself in good health with plenty of energy to work, spend time with family, and stay creative. Self-care is not a luxury; it's a necessity. Your body and health determine your performance in the game and your business. Pay attention to the signals your body sends you. Are you tired? Take a break if necessary. Feeling stressed? Practice breathing techniques. Your well-being is a state you can control by prioritizing it.

- ❖ **Time:** Taking your time seriously is a level of self-care. Consider where you are spending it. In a game that only lasts 24 hours, with 8 hours spent sleeping, use the remaining 16 hours wisely. Waking up early can start the day ahead with no distractions, already feeling productive. However, find whatever routine works for you and be efficient with your timing.

- ❖ **Energy:** We are energy, and where you spend your time is where you spend your energy. Remember, you have the control to say no and prioritize yourself. If you feel like it's time to reset energy-wise, try grounding— recharging through nature. Go outside, touch the grass, breathe pure air, and disconnect from stress. I do this activity alone or with close people because if we are energetic, we shouldn't be with everyone but with those who make us feel like family.

Practice Self-Care

- ◆ **Regular Exercise:** You don't need to become a gym rat. A simple daily walk or quick home workout can do wonders for your physical and mental health, enabling you to perform at a higher peak.

- ❖ **Healthy Eating:** Fuel your body with the right nutrients. It's not about dieting; it's about making sustainable, healthy choices. Eliminate carbs that slow you down. Do your research and try different things to check your performance.

- ❖ **Adequate Sleep:** Your body needs time to recharge. Aim for 7-8 hours of quality sleep each night to keep your energy levels full for the next day's challenges.

- ❖ **Practice Mindfulness:** Incorporate moments of mindfulness into your day. Whether through meditation, deep breathing, or a hobby you enjoy, take time to unwind. Find a place where you can relax from stressful situations. Listen within, with zero distractions, just prioritizing your thoughts because they are powerful in making anything happen. It has to be in your mind first to become your reality.

- ❖ **Set Boundaries:** Learn to say no when necessary. Setting boundaries protects your time and energy from being drained. If you have your priorities clear, this shouldn't be an issue.

Conclusion

Balancing work and life in this game is not rocket science. It's about being mindful of your well-being, managing your time wisely, and realizing that success is not just about reaching the destination but enjoying the journey along the way. So, level up your life by finding that sweet spot of balance!

Your Thoughts:

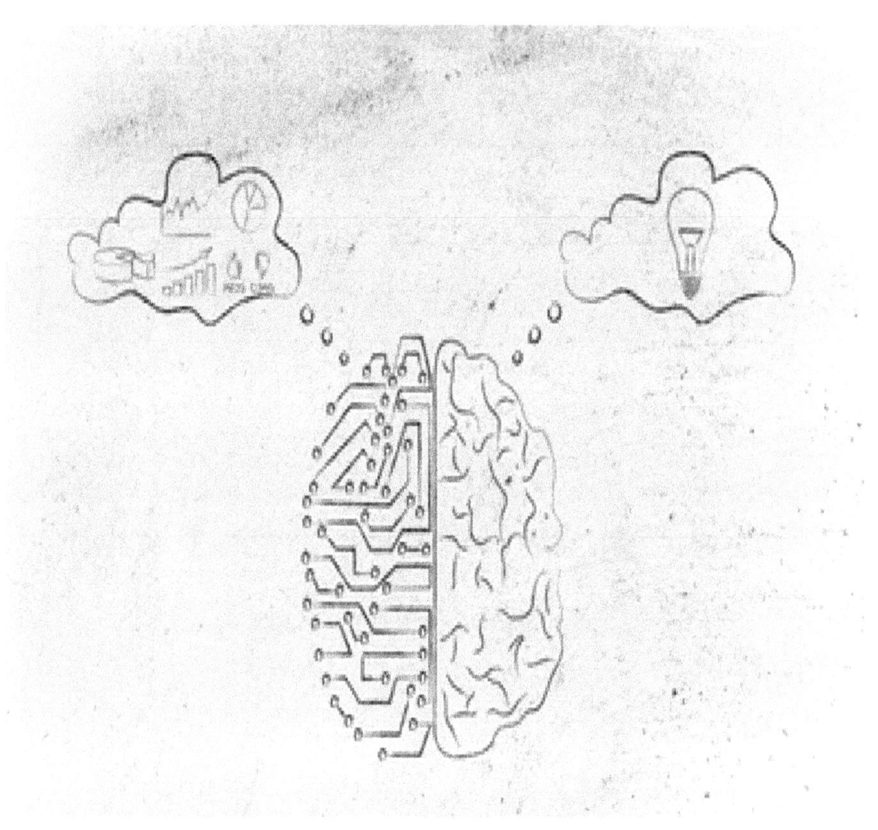

RES DATA

CHAPTER ELEVEN - CREATIVITY

The Power Of Creativity In This Game

Imagine creativity as your weapon, propelling you forward in The Game. It's not just about thinking outside the box; it's about realizing there is no box. Being able to create takes you from being a passive consumer to an active player in your narrative by going to stores and analyzing to get creative on how you would optimize it or make it effective for the franchise. One thing about imagination is that there's no limit to how much you can create; you are either a creator or a consumer, so you will have to decide which one you want to be.

Creating Alone With My Thoughts

The creator journey begins when you allow your mind to wander freely, unburdened by external opinions. In this space, your mind becomes a canvas, ready to write your own story and stop reading everyone else's because, as creators, we create no matter what our environment's opinions are. Remember, nobody else's opinion matters at this stage—it's all about letting your thoughts flow.

The only way to be a successful creator is to let your thoughts flow and embrace the work that you do. Nothing matters, so just focus on enjoying the process by yourself. Eventually, you will have people support it because there's an audience for everything out there; just be you. Our minds are powerful for creating, and we should take advantage of it by spending more time creating than consuming.

The Simple Way

1. **Go For A Walk With A Notepad:** One of the most accessible methods to enhance creativity is a simple walk armed with nothing but a notepad. Nature, whether it's the soothing waves at the beach or the rustling leaves in a park provides a backdrop that encourages your mind to explore. Find a safe and peaceful spot away from distractions, and let your mind wander freely.

2. This is not easy for some people, but I encourage you to go out for a walk anywhere you feel peace of mind, away from humanity, just by yourself. There, you can listen to your thoughts, write them down, start putting them together, and create.

3. This could be a new business idea, a book that you would like to write, content creation, a new project or anything that your mind tells you to try out. It would also be a way to create new ideas for improving existing projects.

- **Create Your Safe Thinking Space**

1. Identify a physical or mental space where you feel safe and at ease. It could be a cozy corner in your home, a quiet café, or in a nearby park. This safe space becomes your creative sanctuary, allowing your mind to roam without constraint.

2. A safe space should be where you feel comfortable being by yourself or with a friend who is willing to listen to your thoughts out loud and brainstorm about it; as I mentioned before, the mind is super powerful, and that's how we create our reality. A man comes in with an idea and desire to get it done; after you have everything together, it's your responsibility to make it possible, but you already have the plan by doing the work of listening to your powerful mind.

My Excelled Story Through Creativity

1. Let's take a page from Glen's playbook. Like many others, delved into the mysteries of the mind. I realized the untapped potential residing in the unconscious mind. By understanding the depth of my thoughts and leveraging the wealth of information within, I elevated my game in both personal and professional realms.

2. I started being curious about the mind when I started entrepreneurship because I figured we have control of our success if we have control of our mind, so I started learning about the subconscious mind by trying psychedelics like a ceremony to dig inside my mind to find out information we only have reach in a high-frequency state, the mind opens up like a book full of information that will make you realize how you have gotten where you are and why. I got an expensive mentor to do Neuro-feedback in my brain to optimize my thinking, decision making and creativity to learn in-depth about my mind. Hence, I discovered the different flow states we have and how to trigger them.

3. I'm always talking about the mind and how powerful it is. You can really achieve anything you think about if you really don't let go of the belief that you can achieve the idea that will become a reality only if you take action, be persistent and never give up on those ideas by being creative, trying and trying over and over, Here you go that's literally the secret of accomplishing your desires. Still, it's more complex than when you have a weak mindset and you are your main obstacle, not even people's opinions. So, coming back to my story, I started working on my mindset first because I understood it was the foundation of my success.

A Note For Beginners

If you're new to the game of creativity, start small. Take short walks, jot down your thoughts, and gradually expand your creative playground. Remember, there are no rules – only possibilities waiting to be discovered.

Creativity is not a talent reserved for a select few; it's a skill waiting to be cultivated. As you start on this journey of unleashing your creativity, embrace the joy of creation, relish the process and watch how it transforms your game in the most remarkable ways. Get ready to be amazed by the wonders your mind can create.

Your Thoughts:

1.
2.
3.
CHANGE
ADJUST
MODIFY
NEW
SHIFT
TRANSITION
TRANSFORM

CHAPTER TWELVE - ADAPT TO CHANGE

The Inevitability Of Change

Change is a constant, an undeniable force that shapes the narrative of our lives. While stepping into the unknown might feel uncomfortable, embracing change opens the door to success in this game. Life is full of surprises, and being prepared for the unexpected is a game-changer.

It's inevitable not to adapt when we, as human beings, are constantly evolving in the game while we figure out who we are and who we want to become. So adaptability is a skill you want to master in this game; some of you have the prestige of living a good life where your parents take care of everything, but if you aren't ready to adapt, you might be in trouble.

Getting Comfortable With Discomfort

Change often brings discomfort, and let's face it—being uncomfortable is not the most pleasant experience. However, it's in these moments of discomfort that we find the seeds of personal growth. Think of it as leveling up in the game. Just like facing a challenging boss in a game, embracing discomfort in real life is the key to unlocking new levels and success.

Being able to adapt to any situation will give you a hidden power and the ability to take more risks, knowing that you can adapt to the situations coming your way and succeed afterward. Remember, this game is not only about winning but also about learning while you gain XP, making yourself uncomfortable. Let's be honest; nobody wants to be uncomfortable, but it pays off once you adapt to it.

Strategies To Embrace Discomfort

1. **Try New Things:**

- Break the routine by trying activities outside your comfort zone. It could be something as simple as trying new cuisine, picking up a new hobby, or exploring a different part of town, but just try to do new activities, in general, to discover how far you can take yourself.

- For example, when I started entrepreneurship, it was quite hard to talk to strangers, like literally somebody new in a meeting, and make a connection, so I started reading about it, like "How to Win Friends and Influence people." This is like Networking 101, so I also started believing I already do this by repeating to myself day in and day out: "I'm a master communicator," and "I connect with people easily all the time." Then I had the confidence and knowledge of how to do it, then now, naturally by being interested in the other person by asking them questions & being genuinely curious, it sounds easy, right, but at first takes some guts to get out of the comfort zone and do it.

2. **Talk to Strangers:**

- Engage in conversations with people you wouldn't typically approach. New perspectives and connections often emerge from these unexpected interactions, like going to a meeting you have never been to before, which could be for networking, business, webinar or anything related to what you do.

- You will target those individuals who look like the leaders and guard them down by being interested in them genuinely to keep things real and enjoy the conversation. You wait until they get curious to ask about you; at this point, it's your time to shine because each person is an opportunity for you to elevate your game completely. Be ready for an introduction of yourself or have been looking for a partnership and a place to do it or maybe a mentor if you can provide value.

3. Step Out from The Normal Routine:

- Routines can be comforting, but they can also be limiting. Shake things up by altering your daily habits and decisions. Take a different route to work, try a different workout, or change your morning routine instead of looking at the phone and touching the grass; feel grateful for what you have or simply write it down; just think about it if you do the same over and over, you will get the same result over and over.

- It might not be easy, but it is said that being successful is about discovering your highest potential by pushing yourself to do things you never thought of. This means waking up and switching things up, like the way you talk to yourself or the habits you currently have. Question yourself daily about your results to see if you are where you want to be and where there's room for improvement.

4. Embrace Uncomfortable Situations:

- Challenge yourself to tackle situations that make you uneasy. It could be public speaking, taking on a leadership role, or anything that pushes your boundaries because this is the only way you can get to experience that high potential I'm talking about only if you really want to be the best version of yourself.

- "Being uncomfortable is fun for me because I always get a story out of it and experience it, so I really enjoy it now going through things that used to embarrass me." It wasn't easy at all to get uncomfortable over and over again to the point I get uncomfortable daily, and I push myself as nobody will; I'm the only person with me 24/7, and if I can push myself, who will do it the same way all day long?

Stories Of Thriving In Change

Despite being a reader who enjoys solitude, I have recognized the value of networking in diverse environments. At the same time, you have a clear vision to attract and connect with the right people. I transformed my daily routine by networking at the gym, restaurants, and anywhere I found myself. By stepping out of my comfort zone, I forged connections that enriched my personal and professional life.

Additionally, I venture into yoga, a departure from my usual activities, showcasing my commitment to embracing change. Starting with a simple desire to feel better physically, I found myself challenging my limits, stretching beyond my comfort zone both mentally and physically. Still, I concluded that this is a lifestyle by being an entrepreneur or creator; at least the successful ones embrace change as part of their lifestyle.

In "Embracing Change," The Game of Life becomes more fulfilling when we accept the inevitability of change. Through discomfort and uncertainty, opportunities for growth and success emerge. The change is not the end of the game but a thrilling new level waiting to be conquered.

Your Thoughts:

CHAPTER THIRTEEN - VISUALIZATION POWERS

Understanding Visualization

"So what's this visualization thing all about? I call it manifesting; it's the art of creating a mental picture of what I want to achieve." Imagine it as a roadmap to your dreams, a crystal-clear vision of where you're headed.

It's quite simple."In religion, one is taught to have faith. I'm telling you how I've achieved my goals by believing in myself since I was 18." It's all thanks to visualizing. When I was certain of what I wanted, I could start talking about it in the present and taking action, positioning myself in the right rooms. There's no secret, but there is belief. If you believe in yourself, it's all you need to be unstoppable.

Finding Yourself And Your Why

Before digging deep into visualization techniques, take a moment to find yourself. What drives you? What's your purpose? Your "why" is the fuel that keeps your engine running. Your vision is not just a goal; it's the ongoing journey of life, a clear picture of how you want to live. There's a bigger purpose in life beyond financial success, something within you that you need to discover. I found mine through isolation and journaling. My purpose is to contribute by empowering others, which is why if you meet me, I will make sure to provide value to you.

Money alone isn't enough to keep us going on days when we don't feel like it. I can't rely solely on motivation because, like everyone else, I get tired and sad. There are days I don't want to train, but I have something bigger than a goal: a purpose. To truly contribute, I need to lead and to lead others, I need to lead myself.

Techniques For Visualizing Goals

1. **Start With Clarity:** Every project has goals, systems, and more, but the vision is your game plan. Picture it like creating a mental movie. What's happening? How are you feeling? The more vivid, the better. It has to be a big feeling that gives you goosebumps every time you think about it, making it feel like your responsibility to get it done.

2. **Create A Vision Board:** If you're a visual learner, consider making a vision board. It's like crafting a poster of your goals using images and words. Place it where you can see it daily for a quick reminder. Cut some pictures from a magazine or print out your vision and how you see yourself in the future. For example, I have images of my family, representing the family I'm building with my fiancée and the houses. I need many keys to own many houses, so I have pictures of the keys. I also want to provide for the family that raised me. Try it yourself.

The Connection Between Visualization And Achievement

1. **Break It Down:** Here's the real secret sauce. While daydreaming is fantastic, breaking down your vision into achievable steps is where the magic happens. Turn your big picture into bite-sized pieces.

- Daily habits or activities are essential for achieving your goals. Highlight what you shouldn't do and eliminate it from your subconscious mind. It will help you take responsibility for accomplishing small steps every day, even when nobody's watching.

2. **Daily Activities For The Win:** A vision without action is just a pretty thought. Your daily activities should align with your vision. Each step takes you closer to your goal. Remember, taking action is the most crucial part.

3. It serves as a bridge from dreams to reality, focusing on what you can control, like daily actions. Don't stress over situations you can't control. If there's nothing you can do about it. Let it be.

Visualization In Action: Glen's Story

Let's peek into my world. My vision was to create a business that thrived financially and made a positive impact. My mental movie included scenes of contributing to others, building connections, and supporting causes close to my heart. That's why I collaborate with so many people. Contrary to what the system teaches us, we are stronger together.

Techniques I Used:

- I visualized specific scenarios, like closing successful deals or seeing my business name on the first page of Google. Then, I took the time to learn the necessary skills, like SEO; for example, my business ranked #1 because I visualized it and took action.

- My vision board featured images representing my goals, from a thriving business to the causes I support.

Achievement Through Visualization:

I didn't stop at visualizing; I broke down my vision into daily tasks. Each day, I aligned my actions with my mental picture, moving steadily toward my goals. By aiming for 1% growth each day, I made my dreams achievable with consistency. I woke up earlier to have time to write this book, transforming the idea into reality.

Conclusion

Visualization is not just wishful thinking; it's a roadmap to success. Find your vision, make it crystal clear, and turn it into actionable steps. As we move forward in our journey, keep this powerful tool in mind. Get ready to visualize your way to success!

Your Thoughts:

ATTITUDE
BEHAVIOUR
MINDSET
ACTION
SOLUTION
RESULTS
PERFORMANCE

CHAPTER FOURTEEN - THE MINDSET OF SUCCESS

The Power Of Your Mindset:

In this game of life, your mindset is your key to success—your operating system. Picture it as the software that runs in the background, influencing every decision and action you take. Developing a growth mindset is crucial. What does that mean? It's about believing in your ability to improve and succeed, seeing challenges as opportunities to grow, and understanding that your efforts can lead to mastery over time.

Train your mindset by learning how it works, reading, and being disciplined on a continuous daily basis. Improvement comes with discipline and curiosity to learn more and go to the next level. Life can be seen as a complex and ever-evolving game. The battlefield lies not in the external world but within the realm of the mind. Just like any game, the key to mastery lies in our ability to make strategic decisions, adapt to challenges and remain steadfast in our pursuits.

To dominate this mental game, we must take control of our thoughts, steer them with purpose, and maintain consistency in our actions. Growth often resides in the discomfort of pushing beyond our limits, forcing us to confront and overcome our fears and doubts. By embracing the uncomfortable and viewing each obstacle as an opportunity to level up, we can continuously evolve, becoming stronger, wiser, and more resilient with each step. In this relentless pursuit of mental mastery, we unlock the potential to shape our reality and achieve the extraordinary.

Strategies For A Positive And Resilient Mindset

Now, let's discuss basic strategies for leveling up your mindset. First, practice affirmations. These are positive statements you repeat to yourself to build confidence and focus. Imagine your mind as a garden—affirmations are like planting seeds of positivity. Nurture them daily, and you'll see a flourishing mindset. However, don't forget to take action as well. It's not enough to tell yourself you look good; you also need to hit the gym and boost that confidence to the roof.

Another key strategy is keeping your promises to yourself. If you say you'll do something, follow through. It builds trust in yourself and reinforces a can-do attitude. Setting big goals is fantastic, but the real magic happens when you break them into smaller, manageable steps. Each small step completed is a victory, propelling you forward.

Stories Of Mindset Transformation

Let's look at real-life players who transformed their mindset and achieved success. Take my journey, for instance. I wanted to be physically stronger, so I committed to going to the gym every day. It seemed daunting at first, but by being consistent and breaking down the challenge into smaller tasks, I gradually achieved my goal. The same principles apply in business and life—consistency and breaking down big goals into achievable steps.

Consider others who've transformed their mindset. There's the entrepreneur who started with a simple idea, faced setbacks, but maintained a growth mindset, turning those setbacks into stepping stones. Or the individual who committed to learning a new skill faced challenges but persisted, eventually mastering the skill.

Conclusion

The mindset of success is within your grasp. Develop a growth mindset, practice affirmations, keep your promises to yourself and witness the transformation in your life. Remember, success in the game isn't reserved for a select few—it's a journey anyone can start on. So, set your mindset for success, believe in yourself, and get ready to conquer the challenges ahead. The game is yours to win!

<table>
<tr><td>Your Thoughts:</td></tr>
<tr><td></td></tr>
<tr><td></td></tr>
<tr><td></td></tr>
<tr><td></td></tr>
<tr><td></td></tr>
<tr><td></td></tr>
</table>

CHAPTER FIFTEEN - NAVIGATING RELATIONSHIPS AND EMBRACING THEM FOR A LIFETIME

The Relationship Rules: More Than Just Networking Or Getting Contacts

In this game of life, relationships are the power-ups that can propel you to new levels of success. It's not just about networking; it's about building genuine connections with people. Why? Because when trust is established, business opportunities follow suit.

Understanding who you're building a relationship with is crucial. Not every connection aligns with your goals, and that's okay. Choose your allies wisely. Make sure your relationships complement your vision, creating a synergy that benefits both parties.

Strategies for Relationship Mastery

Building and maintaining healthy relationships doesn't have to be rocket science. Here are some simple strategies that even a dummy can grasp:

- **Be Genuine and Authentic:** Just be yourself. Authenticity builds trust. People appreciate sincerity, and when you're genuine, it's easier for others to connect with you.

- By being genuinely interested in somebody and listening to them until they get curious about you, then it is time to be prepared for your presentation. For example, I have different presentations depending on what business or resource I want to promote or provide, depending on their needs. Then you need interesting stories like I have so many I could talk for hours, but I don't get attached to it. Just add up a story if you have an interesting one so the person gets more comfortable sharing one with you as well.

- **Show Interest:** Be genuinely interested in others. Ask questions, listen actively, and show that you care. Everyone loves to feel important and be heard. For example, I would ask more questions about the current topic, be curious about them, and get to know each other.

- **Let Them Be Curious About You:** Relationships are a two-way street. While you're interested in others, leave room for them to be curious about you. Share your story, but only spill some of the beans at a time. Keep them intrigued but amazed by your way of presenting yourself.

Success Stories: Who Mastered Relationships

Now, let's look at some real-life players who leveraged relationships for success. Take me, for example. I supported my friend who owns a restaurant by being a loyal customer. This not only strengthened our friendship but also created a business relationship. When I needed a venue for an event, I had a reliable connection with my friend Pedro.

Another instance involves a friend running a marketing agency. I invested in my social media strategy with them, aligning their expertise with my vision. This not only boosted my online presence but also contributed to the success of my goals because I became a partner in the company to meet more individuals and share with people my experience in social media marketing. So, I invested in a relationship that also helped me obtain the skill to market anything online.

These examples highlight the power of relationships when leveraged strategically. By supporting friends in their ventures, I not only strengthened our bonds but also created a network of valuable resources that aligned with my vision and goals for the future.

In conclusion, navigating relationships in the game of life is about more than just shaking hands and exchanging business cards. It's about building meaningful connections, being authentic, showing interest in others, and strategically aligning your relationships with your goals. So, gear up and level up your relationship game – it might just be the key to your next big win!

Your Thoughts:

CHAPTER SIXTEEN: DISCOVER YOUR HIDDEN POTENTIAL

Understanding Hidden Potential

Let's start with a simple truth: we often underestimate ourselves. Sometimes, we believe we're good at something just because it's familiar or we've been doing it for a while. The reality is that with enough time and practice, you can become proficient in almost anything. Your hidden potential lies dormant until you tap into your higher self. The key is to get to know yourself so well that you unleash a version of yourself that is truly unstoppable.

Nobody teaches us about this game better than ourselves. Self-education is the best way to discover your potential by figuring out what you excel at and what you enjoy doing. It involves learning about everything but niching down to what you are good at and enjoy.

To put this in perspective, we come into this world without choosing our name or lifestyle. By the time you're reading this, I hope you understand that you are in control of your life and the results you get. Through the process of success development, you will face many obstacles and often find your hidden potential when you step out of your comfort zone and deal with pressure to find your diamond inside.

Discovering Personal Strengths

From the time we were kids, we've been trying out new things, discovering what we like and what we don't. Personal strengths aren't always obvious and can even hide in the things you might not like about yourself. It's about flipping the perspective and realizing that your uniqueness can be a strength. One of the most powerful tool you possess is your brain. It's your biggest strength, and understanding how it works is the gateway to unlocking your full potential.

Think about it: we all have a brain that controls our decisions, meaning we control the outcome. Take time to reflect on the power you have. Once you realize it and prove to yourself that you are powerful. There's no going back to normal. Understanding how the brain communicates through neural signals we produce in a frequency can help you program your mind. By maintaining a high frequency while thinking or speaking about your goals in the present, you can believe them and then obtain them.

Being by yourself is the best way to connect with your higher self so you can make better decisions for yourself instead of searching for external answers. Everything you are looking for is inside of you. Silence your environment and just listen to your thoughts in a quiet, safe place so you can concentrate on the decisions you make.

Imagine how many decisions we make every day while playing this game. If you take a moment to analyze with your gut or whatever you believe in—some call it God, others Allah, but I believe in myself and my brain—you can focus on the energy you put towards something. Believe in yourself and what you are working on. Don't worry about failure because it will happen, and it's the best thing ever because we learn from it and become stronger. I actually love failing as much as I love winning.

The Power Of The Mindset

In my journey, I initially believed my potential was in sports. While I still enjoy sports, I discovered that the real game-changer was my mind. The mind is an incredible powerhouse capable of storing and accessing unlimited information. To unlock your potential, understanding the workings of your mind is crucial. I am here to guide you through my process that can help you harness the incredible power of your mindset.

Everything starts changing once you change your mindset and beliefs about self-worth. Sometimes, we sabotage ourselves, preventing us from reaching higher levels. Put this in perspective: we could all make our dreams come true if we stopped sabotaging ourselves in every single decision we make. This goes back to the mind.

In my personal experience, I have always figured things out by operating from the right mindset and being efficient. I have the power of problem-solving, no matter what it is. I always stay positive and figure something out. For example, the first time I crashed or was betrayed by a business partner, my mindset was to just move forward. There was nothing else to do but go forward, analyze the next steps, and figure out how to reduce the chances of such situations happening again.

Stories Of Unlocked Potential

To bring these concepts to life, let me share a personal story. As a child, I believed my potential was limited to sports. However, as I plunged into understanding my mind, everything changed. I learned how to retain more information, and access it at will, and use it for my benefit. The mind is a tool that can be either a powerful ally or a formidable adversary. The choice is yours, and I'm here to share with you the path to harnessing its unlimited potential.

Hard work is fine, but the ultimate goal is to work smart by analyzing and providing feedback without losing it. Control your mind to avoid making bad decisions that interrupt your progress. Allow your creative ideas to navigate situations while you keep evolving in the game. Be the main character, and you will enjoy it completely, even during the hard times. Think of it as a mental game.

Since I changed my beliefs during a retreat, my mom took me to Colombia, and I've approached situations differently.

Now, I always look for the good side and keep going. The whole mindset idea is that if I fall, I will pick myself up and keep going until I get what I want. Every day, I wake up with a desire because I want freedom and peace of mind. I achieved that because I was willing to pick myself up as many times as needed.

In the next chapters, we'll explore practical methods for unlocking your hidden potential and share more stories of individuals who have unlocked their latent strengths. Remember, you have a reservoir of untapped abilities within you, and together, we'll discover how to set them free.

Your Thoughts:

CHAPTER SEVENTEEN - FACING ADVERSITY

Adversity 101: It's Okay, You're Learning

Imagine you're the creator of the game, and you've been playing for a while. You know the ins and outs. But suddenly, a new challenge appears. Maybe it's a tricky client or a problem with an order. The thing is, facing adversity is normal, especially when you're leveling up and doing things you've never done before.

So, here's the deal: Adversity is your in-game teacher. It's okay to have only some of the answers right away. Every challenge is a chance to learn and grow. Consider it a lesson in the game of life, and trust me, you'll probably come out of it with some valuable skills.

If you have the strength to pick yourself up when adversity throws you down, it means that you can go through these challenges by yourself and rise by yourself. You don't have to do it alone, but it means that you realize you don't need anybody to pick you up because you have the strength to learn from every setback and actually grow from these situations. When we lose is really when we are learning and growing, so I highly suggest you enjoy the setbacks.

Overcoming Adversity: The How-To Guide

Now, let's talk about overcoming adversity. It's like having a secret weapon in your arsenal and that secret weapon is a strong mindset. There's no magic spell or cheat code for overcoming challenges, but with the right mindset, you can face anything.

We need to adapt to situations without letting someone step on us. Still, situations, where it's clearly making us sad or something related to you where you have your feelings involved are really the hard ones, like a partnership betrayal because usually, that partner is a family member or a close person you trust to go into business. By getting the mindset ready to be resilient in those situations and work on yourself when those setbacks arrive, not by drinking or hanging out avoiding situations but by confronting them and learning how not to do it.

1. **Learn and Grow:**
   - Treat adversity as a lesson. Understand what went wrong and figure out how you can do better next time.

   - Most of the time, when we make a bad decision, our ego is too big, so we don't want to accept it, but really, it is the best way to become better. If you start studying other people's setbacks, trust me, you will learn from others, especially those at the high levels.

2. **Build Mental Strength:**
   - Your mind is your greatest asset. Strengthen it by staying positive, focusing on solutions, and not letting setbacks define you.

   - Practice every day to be ready for the moment. We don't really plan to fail, but we fail to plan. "Read it again."Plan to practice regularly so that when the time comes, you are prepared to shift to the next direction, likely by making a decision and analyzing the situation.

3. **Stay Resilient:**
   - Resilience is like your character's superpower. Use it to bounce back from setbacks, adapt to changes, and keep moving forward.

I can assure you there will be lessons along the way, but the difference between success and failure is how they react to situations, so stay ready.

Real-Life Player

In my own life, I've faced plenty of challenges. Each obstacle became a building block, shaping my character and mindset. When tough situations arise, I'm ready to jab them head-on. Hiding or ignoring problems won't make them disappear.

I have been in really stressful situations where I get paralyzed and cannot think or do anything, but understanding the mind has helped me become stronger and not really freak out about situations that come daily in the game.

Remember, life is already challenging, and our minds can either make it tougher or help us navigate through it. The key is to face adversity, learn from it, and come out stronger on the other side.

So, the next time you encounter a tough level in the game, remember: It's just a part of the adventure. Face it, learn from it, and watch yourself level up. You've got this!

<table>
<tr><td>Your Thoughts:</td></tr>
<tr><td>

</td></tr>
<tr><td>

</td></tr>
<tr><td>

</td></tr>
<tr><td>

</td></tr>
<tr><td>

</td></tr>
<tr><td>

</td></tr>
<tr><td>

</td></tr>
</table>

CHAPTER EIGHTEEN - MASTERING TIME MANAGEMENT

Time: The Real Bank of Life

Imagine this: Time is a bank where you deposit seconds, minutes, and hours. Once a withdrawal is made, there's no going back. In our bustling world, it's easy to overlook the value of these time investments. As you progress, you will find that certain tasks, such as cooking, driving, or handling chores like laundry, can be delegated as transactions.

But why, you may ask? Because in this game, your time is a limited resource, and spending it wisely is the key to progressing to the next level. As you ascend, you'll find that some tasks are better suited for others, allowing you to focus on what truly levels you up.

The time you spend doing laundry or washing the dishes at level one is different at level ten because your time is worth more, so it's smarter to outsource it. That being said, if you are at a low level, do it yourself while you have the time. The idea is to level up to get busy doing things that are worth your time.

There are levels to the game, so it's your responsibility to keep track of your time and how you spend it. Remember, the only way to change a bad habit or an activity draining your time is to notice it first, analyze what you do with your time, and then replace it with the right activities.

Prioritize to Monetize: Building Your Value Empire

Now that you've grasped the concept of time as a currency let's talk about prioritizing tasks. Imagine your to-do list as a treasure map and each task as a potential treasure chest. Your goal is to identify the chests with the most valuable loot—the tasks that align with your goals and vision.

As you gain experience, you'll learn that not all tasks are created equal. Some require your unique skills. Others can be entrusted to the NPCs (Non-Playable Characters) in your life, gradually building an ecosystem where your time is invested in high-value activities. The result? Increased productivity and a character progression worthy of your epic saga.

We often have excuses for the results we get, but we also have excuses when it comes to doing the activities nobody wants to do to achieve those results. It's a matter of priorities. If you really want that car, you work and get it. If you want to travel, you plan it out and get it. It's your priority. It would help if you looked at what's aligned with your vision and what you are doing to get closer to it.

Every second you spend on your activities makes you better and better. So why not use the time wisely for what's actually on your mind? Remember to delay gratification: suffer now to get the result later.

Time: The Magic Elixir of Success

In the enchanting world of entrepreneurship, starting a business or pursuing any goal requires time. It's the magic elixir that fuels your learning, experimentation, and occasional missteps. As you navigate the game, having an abundance of time is akin to having a backpack full of potions that enhance your skills and attributes. It provides you with the luxury to stretch your mind, acquire new skills, and turn your aspirations into tangible achievements.

Write things down to get them done. We have too many things in our heads, so make sure you get things done by establishing a routine or adding tasks to your calendar to keep track of your time. Just imagine that when you manage more people, you also manage their time. The way to manage someone's time is by having their calendar and making sure they complete their tasks.

Time doesn't stop, so once I wake up, it's a good feeling to control everything I do without rushing because I wake up early enough. I start my day with extra time to do certain activities and be ahead of the average person. I take the time to count my blessings and do breathwork. I understand my body and energy levels for peak performance, so I spend my mornings working and fasting to be most productive. I take my first meal by 12 pm-1 pm, slowing down since the body needs energy to process food. I spend this time learning or doing light work before working out and continuing with my day.

The Epic Quest

Now, let's explore the epic quest that will transform you into a time management maestro. Grab your notebook (or smartphone), and let's get started:

1. **List Your Quests:** Jot down all the activities you need to conquer. Prioritize your tasks, starting with the hardest ones. Once you accomplish this one, the smaller ones will be easier.

2. **Map Your Priorities:** Identify the quests that lead to the ultimate treasure (your goals). Look at your schedule and try to fit them all in by level of urgency and value.

3. **Summon Your Allies:** Pinpoint quests that can be delegated to your trusty sidekicks. For example, while in school, everything is scheduled for you. Do the same for yourself to educate yourself on certain topics by priority. If you have access to a mentor, outsource learning tasks. For meals, if you have access to a chef, have them prepare healthy food and clean up

after. For me, a chef and a driver are must-haves to allow me to focus on activities worth my time. The mission here is to level up your skills so you can delegate tasks you dislike or are not good at.

4. **Forge Your Value Arsenal:** Eventually, you will have a ton of skills and experience that will serve as currency. Just like I exchange my skills for dollars or time, you can exchange your valuable skills for something of worth. The mission is to learn as many valuable skills as possible for your game.

As you complete this homework quest, you'll not only become a master of time management but also unlock achievements that propel you further in the game of life. So, embark on this quest with enthusiasm, and may your time be forever in your favor!

Your Thoughts:

CHAPTER NINETEEN - PEAK PERFORMANCE

Unlocking Your Superhuman Side: The Consistency Code

Imagine being so consistent that your performance reaches superhuman levels. Well, here's the secret: follow your own rules and stack those days like a champ. Picture it like building a tower of blocks; each day gets you closer to that peak performance zone. The game-changer? Consistency. Stick to your game plan, and you'll be on your way to almost perfect performance.

Part of becoming superhuman is doing the impossible for the average person, and consistency is one way to keep the momentum up. So whenever you decide to change your life for the better, remember that if you start, you should have it as part of your lifestyle, not just because you feel motivated. Tomorrow is Monday so you will start tomorrow.

Fasting but not only food but fasting needs to be applied to people as well. I believe fasting can get us to peak performance when we balance it out. It is necessary because, at that time, to give us clarity, we should connect with our higher self, "the best version of ourselves," and not underestimate the food. After all, everything we eat is how we are going to perform in the game. So you understand real quick: Carbs will slow you down and convert into fat, but instead of protein, healthy fats will maintain you at peak performance.

Strategies For Everyday Superpowers

Now, let's talk about optimizing your performance and reaching those goals. You don't need a cape; you need a plan. Start with the basics:

1. Exercise and proper nutrition.

2. Think of your body as your trusty sidekick.

3. Treat it well, and it'll help you conquer challenges.

It doesn't have to be complicated—just move around a bit and eat things that grew in the ground. Doing yoga or any type of meditation elevates your brain wave frequencies, just like the monks do. It gets the brain to a peak level where you will attract the answer to whatever you are thinking about or even attract it because that's how powerful the mind is.

Meet Toby, The Brain Wizard Behind "Neuro Flex," My Brain Coach

Ever wish you could optimize your brain, making it work like a well-oiled machine? Meet Toby, the brainiac Founder and Owner of Neuro Flex. It's like a superhero for your brain. Toby's the expert in neuroscience who can help you become more efficient, and trust me, it's incredible how it works. While it sounds like sci-fi, it's actually a practical way to level up your mental game.

I met Toby in the Porsche towel doing one of his brain scans. He is a successful guy, so I started asking questions and doing my research. I have been researching the mind and trying to master it since my mindset shifted to a creator instead of a consumer. So, I started doing the program myself to scan my brain every single day to exercise, level up brain communication, and optimize my mind to peak performance during daily exercises.

Investing In Your Performance: The Brainy Bucks

Sure, brain optimization might sound a tad pricey, but think of it as an investment in your superhero abilities. Imagine paying a little now to unlock exceptional results later. It's like buying the ultimate power-up in a video game—it might cost a few extra coins, but the advantages are totally worth it.

I'm not promoting anything in the book that I haven't tried myself, but I have invested a lot in mentors and experiences, so this is why I have something to tell and so many stories that I don't think are all in the book.

Investing time in the beginning to do your research or learn the free stuff should be the goal of a level one player to level up and get mentors at some point by now investing time and money because the higher the level, the higher the investment you should do on yourself.

Superhuman Exceptional Results :

I don't believe in routines, and I want to say that we all function differently, so it's about finding out what works for you by trying things out.

Well, I will tell you my rules on how I reach peak performance by, first of all, starting my day grateful for the most meaningful things to me, like my family. Then I don't eat anything until 1-2 pm to have the body in survival mode and have my energy and attention on one thing since the stomach takes a lot of energy from me then I only surround myself with winners that become better 1% better everyday meaning people who talk about success and positive words then I keep the momentum up by winning and being consistent. At the same time, the average person rests and enjoys the weekend. I always get ahead by doing the simple stuff I mentioned above.

Take this from my personal experience: I'm a human just like you, and I make mistakes as well because I will never be perfect. But if I'm growing 1% a day and I keep the consistency going, that will compound so much in a few years, just like Warren Buffet did with his money.

Everyone has the potential to get their superhuman out because I'm sure you know how to feel at peak performance. Still, the brain plays games to the temptations of trash food or trashy friends, so definitely be aware that we have the power to succeed and the power to put obstacles in front of our way to become superhuman.

So, whether you're aiming for superhero-level consistency, optimizing your brain with Toby's witchcraft, or just curious about the real-life heroes who've walked this path, this chapter is your guide. Peak performance isn't reserved for the elite—it's a game anyone can play. Ready to level up? Let's go to the next.

<table>
<tr><td>Your Thoughts:</td></tr>
<tr><td></td></tr>
<tr><td></td></tr>
<tr><td></td></tr>
<tr><td></td></tr>
<tr><td></td></tr>
<tr><td></td></tr>
</table>

MAX
LEVEL
MIN

CHAPTER TWENTY - THE HIGHEST LEVEL

Welcome to the grand finale of "The Glitch: Escaping The Average." As we reach the climax of this transformative reading, let's dive deeper into the essence of achieving peak performance by mastering the mindset. In the game of life, your mindset is the ultimate power-up, the key that unlocks doors to unparalleled success.

That being said, you need to understand that the game is about leveling up all the time. There's no final level or finish line until we die, so it's our responsibility to become wiser and stronger every day by simply getting uncomfortable doing the activities we are trying to avoid.

Embracing The Unending Journey

This chapter marks not just the conclusion of a book but the commencement of a new chapter in your ongoing saga. Life, much like a captivating game, unfolds endlessly, offering opportunities for growth and self-discovery. Recognize this moment not as an endpoint but as a launchpad to embrace the unending journey that life presents.

Life throws obstacles at us all the time, and society has made us soft by calling it bad times or being unlucky. Most people need to understand that under pressure, diamonds are made. Now, you have a story to tell. Now, your life is interesting because you went to hell and came back. That's the name of the game. Being a glitch means creating my own rules and doing it my way because, as I said, the system makes us soft, but it can all change if you decide to be a glitch in your game.

The Timeless Nature Of Life

Life doesn't adhere to conventional endings; it's a timeless continuum filled with moments waiting to be seized. Every second counts, and in the pursuit of success, it's essential to find joy in the simple things—nature, family, and the solace of your own company. Success isn't solely about financial gains or relentless improvement; it's about finding balance and relishing the beauty in the ordinary.

As men, we must sacrifice for our family and loved ones and set aside time to enjoy the simple things in life, like dinner or some intimate time with our partner. Balance the person you want to become with the person you are today by building yourself for the future. We have nothing to prove to anyone but ourselves because we have full control of our lives by making the right decisions.

The Final Levels: Challenges and Rewards

As you ascend to the final level, envision it as the culmination of your efforts where the challenges aren't small mistakes anymore. At this level, you must be careful with the words you speak and every decision you make. A critical realization dawns at this stage – the need to close your circle and build an ecosystem of winners. Challenges include discerning the trustworthiness of those around you. Envy and support coexist, making it paramount to invest in relationships wisely. The network you've cultivated becomes indispensable, evolving beyond mere connections to chosen family—individuals who share your goals and mindset.

Mastering Your Mindset

Now, let's delve into the heart of peak performance—mastering your mindset. Your mindset is the architect of your reality, shaping your thoughts, actions, and ultimately, your destiny. Embrace a growth mindset that perceives challenges as opportunities and failures as stepping stones toward success. Cultivate resilience, adaptability, and a positive outlook as you navigate the intricate game of life.

It's key to getting uncomfortable every day doing what you're supposed to do. The mind will tell you to relax after work, but your higher self is waiting for you to pick up a book, go for a run, or do public speaking. Get out of your comfort zone to break the patterns of failure. Build patterns of success through your actions and keep your word to yourself. Let's build new patterns.

The Reflection: Living Your Life

As we close this chapter and reflect on the entire book, the revelation is clear: live your life—not your family's or your friends', but yours. Channel your focus into the present task, even when it involves the less glamorous work you'd rather avoid. This is the moment to take action, to level up not only in your professional pursuits but in the very essence of your being.

Growth is about feedback, and sometimes, you need to sit down and give feedback to yourself. Realize the patterns so you can change them to align with the highest version of yourself. I know a lot of people in business who are older than I am, but I'm more successful because I'm constantly giving myself feedback to check my alignment.

"The Glitch: Escaping The Average": A Lifelong Guide

This book is more than a collection of pages; it's a guide, a mentor nudging you toward your highest version. There's an identity of yours that you haven't met yet, and I know this because even for me, there's always a better version of me that I didn't know but work every single day. Your journey doesn't end here; it's a continuous cycle of growth, challenges, and victories.

Armed with the wisdom gained from this book and life lessons, step confidently into the next chapter. Life's game is in your hands, and it's time to play it, savor it, and, above all, keep leveling up. Embrace the adventure with open arms, for "The Glitch in the Game" is your companion in the lifelong quest for excellence.

Your Thoughts:

Dear Starter Player's,

The game of entrepreneurship is hard, just like being comfortable at a 9-to-5 job, but you have to decide wisely and create value for the marketplace to reward you. This book is for those starting who need to know the principal values of the game. There's way more than this because there are levels to this, but starting by working on your mindset and skill acquisition is your starting point.

I recommend learning sales and marketing to get leads for those leads you are acquiring while you level up. It's crucial to make cash flow and build an investing portfolio for long-term goals like real estate, funds or crypto. In the community, you will be able to learn more in-depth about these types of assets.

Remember, this is the only investment that can match the income potential of your business. The return on investment here is always unlimited. So, it's wise to consider these types of investments only when your business has reached the ultimate level of cash flow and performance.

Thank you for the future glitch.

www.ingramcontent.com/pod-product-compliance
Lightning Source LLC
Chambersburg PA
CBHW041812110726
48006CB00019B/2362